cristina's

of sun valley

cristina's
of sun valley

Cristina Ceccatelli Cook

foreword by Renée Behnke
photography by Kirsten Shultz

Gibbs Smith, Publisher
Salt Lake City

A special thank you to my chef, Patrick Jam, and to all my staff.

First Edition
09 08 07 06 05   5 4 3 2 1

Published by
Gibbs Smith, Publisher
P.O. Box 667
Layton, Utah 84041

Orders: 1.800.748.5439
www.gibbs-smith.com

Photographs by Kirsten Shultz: www.kirstenshultz.com
Designed by Drew Furlong: www.drewfurlong.com

Printed and bound in China
Library of Congress Cataloging-in-Publication Data

Cook, Cristina Ceccatelli
    Cristina's of Sun Valley / by Cristina Ceccatelli Cook;
    foreword by Renée Behnke; photography by Kirsten Shultz—1st ed.
    p. cm.
    Includes index.

    ISBN 0-9726585-1-3 (Watson Press ed.)
    ISBN 1-4236-0048-7 (Gibbs Smith, Publisher, ed.)

    1. Cookery—Idaho—Sun Valley.
    2. Cristina's Restaurant.   I. Title.

    TX715.C75894 2005   641.5'09796'32
    QB104-200347

For my parents, Emilio and Gioconda.
As my father always tells me, "Ringraziamo il Signore
per aver buttato via lo stampo dopo la tua nascita."

contents

foreword

Many of us first met Cristina in Sun Valley, Idaho, over ten years ago. Even then she was bringing her passion to the table by presenting her perfect loaves of bread in baskets mounded high. She inherited her strong Italian family traditions, remembering the importance of simple presentation. Her seasonal fare, always the freshest, helped Cristina bless many tables. She is one of those special people in life who is able to combine a love of family, food, and friends by bringing all together to share a moment in time.

Her intuitive cleverness in knowing what we would all like—coconut cookies, perfect bean soup, or roasted chicken—is beautifully balanced by a unique and practical approach that makes entertaining less daunting.

I have been fortunate to have had many opportunities to eat food prepared by Cristina and her talented crew, and to see her in action. Cristina's hands touch every dish, and her love of presentation is evident in everything she prepares. I have watched her put on an event for hundreds while still running a restaurant and take-out facility. The biggest challenge for the many residents and visitors of this wonderful mountain town is how to get a reservation at Cristina's for lunch after a morning of skiing or a great summer hike.

This book is a reflection of a life rich in tradition and culture. Cristina was born in the hills of Florence and shares here not only the beautiful recipes of her homeland, but also the special creations she has adapted for our enjoyment. *Cristina's of Sun Valley* is a book of artistry, photographed and presented so that we may all dream.

Thank you, Cristina, for enriching all our lives through the food we share.

—Renée Behnke
President, Sur La Table

The hills of Florence are my hills....

I was born outside of Florence, in the Valdarno, on La Fattoria di Riofi. It was the estate of my father's father, whom I never knew. I grew up there with my mother and father, my sister and two brothers, my Nonna Elisa and Nonno Lanzi, my Aunt Nella and Aunt Anna and their husbands, and my three cousins.

We lived on the top of a hill in a three-story, pale-yellow house with green shutters, lots of chimneys, and a pigeon coop on the roof. A big stone courtyard was flanked by a chapel on one side and a billiard room on the other. Outside was a pond filled with goldfish, a greenhouse with lemon trees in huge terra cotta pots, and gardens of azaleas, hydrangeas, and fragrant roses.

The billiard room became a little school of five grades for seventeen of us. The teacher biked from town to our house every day. We loved her because she was young and maybe pretty, and she was considered a part of the family. Our cook, Laura, used to bring us midmorning snacks of warm biscotti with crème anglaise, *pane degli angeli* with marmalade, or simply bread with olive oil and parmigiano.

It feels as if it were five hundred years ago, but it was only fifty. The food was simple, satisfying, and fresh from our farm. We grew wheat so we made our own pasta once a week... *come Dio commanda...a mano, con amore.* Eating was about more than just satisfying our hunger. We took time to sit and savor the goodness and colors of life—green olive oil, white bread, and red wine.

Our calendar had seasons, not months. In summer the men worked in the fields harvesting the wheat and corn. The days were long, hot, and dusty, and the cool late afternoons were always welcome. Our family would gather in the garden under the pergola covered with thick grapevines and blooming wisteria. Underneath it was a huge stone table with benches where my father, Emilio, would come from the fields to sit in his work clothes after he had washed his rough hands and splashed his face with cool water from the fountain. On the table were starched linen napkins, red wine, hard cheese, fresh fava beans, white bread, and a sharp, short knife to cut the prosciutto.

Cristina and her father, Emilio (left); Gioconda, Cristina's mother (right)
Cristina's village (top)

13

Hot chores were abandoned as, one by one, we all joined him in the shade. He kept slicing, and we kept eating and sipping the wine mixed with water. My father's feisty, fiery passions cooled to gentle manners. It felt as if time had stopped. Quiet and peaceful, the bees droning above in the wisteria, those were afternoons of pleasant indolence.

Nearby, close to the pergola, we hung our swings from giant holm-oak trees. Our grandmother and aunts would gather to sit in the shade of the oaks to knit, embroider for our trousseaus, shell peas, or prepare tomatoes for the winter sauces. As the women went about their daily rituals, we were secretly listening to them as they laughed and talked. Women talk.

Fall was when we made prosciutto. I hid upstairs and peeked out through the shutters to the courtyard below where my father and the village butcher and the farmers gathered. Fascinated, I watched my father dispatch each pig with one clean shot between the eyes. The butcher would stay with us for weeks, concocting secret aromatic witches' brews to cure the prosciutto, salami, and sausages, which hung in the cold, dark *cantine* for months and months.

In winter we gathered in the large kitchen, in front of fireplaces so tall that you could stand in them. The women would work and talk, plucking the birds that the men had brought home from the hunt. We kids would take turns cranking the wheel to turn the spit as the birds sizzled and popped. Strange, spicy aromas filled the air as we watched the fire fairies fly up the chimney and listened to stories of ghosts and spirits, and what was and was not good for your soul.

On Easter, the neighboring families came to our chapel bearing olive branches and baskets full of hard-boiled eggs to be blessed. The priest and our doctor joined us in our special meal. Gioconda, my beautiful and mysterious mother, would have the chapel decorated with wild purple and pink anemones and pale-blue forget-me-nots we had picked with her in the fields.

Meals were a communion of all five senses. As we took in nourishment, we also took in the people, their faces, laughter and tears—discovering one another in warm, easy companionship. Recipes were passed from one generation to the next, delicious flavors you never tired of. Always the same but always different. Life at La Fattoria di Riofi was one long, delicious dream.

—*Cristina Ceccatelli Cook*

Cristina and her father (left); Cristina and her brother Stefano (right)

appetizers

shrimp toast

makes 20

15 large shrimp, peeled, deveined, and cut into chunks

$^1/_2$ cup green onions, sliced in rounds

$^1/_4$ cup flour

$^1/_4$ cup water

1 egg

1 tablespoon cornstarch

pinch of salt

$^1/_4$ teaspoon white sugar

1 teaspoon sesame oil

white pepper to taste

vegetable oil for frying

5 slices soft, white sandwich bread without crusts, cut in quarters

lime juice (optional)

Preheat oven to 500 degrees.

Prepare a cookie sheet lined with a paper towel.

In a mixing bowl, blend together first 10 ingredients. In a 10-inch saucepan, heat 3 inches of vegetable oil until hot but not smoking. Spoon shrimp mixture onto bread squares a few at a time. Then, using a slotted spoon, place 2 to 3 at a time in the hot oil and cook until light gold in color—about 30 seconds. The toast will flip upside down—gently flip it over. Remove from oil with a slotted spoon and drain on the cookie sheet. Serve hot, drizzled with a few drops of lime juice.

Shrimp toast can be cooked a few hours before serving. In this case, preheat oven to 500 degrees and reheat the toasts until crispy—3 to 5 minutes on the middle shelf.

clams & mussels with a swirl

serves 6 to 8

$2^1/2$ pounds (total) mussels and clams

$1/4$ cup extra virgin olive oil

4 shallots, thinly sliced

4 cloves garlic, thinly sliced

$1/2$ cup chopped sun-dried tomatoes (optional)

2 tablespoons chopped italian parsley

2 bay leaves

$1/4$ cup chopped fresh oregano

$1^1/2$ cups patrick's swirly vinaigrette

salt and pepper to taste

$1/4$ cup chopped basil

1 small bunch chives, chopped

a few whole leaves of parsley

Clean and debeard the mussels and clams. In a large sauté pan, heat the oil, then add shallots and cook for 2 to 3 minutes. Add the garlic, then the clams, mussels, and sun-dried tomatoes. Cook, covered, on very high heat until the shells open, discarding any that do not open. Add parsley, bay leaves, oregano, and the swirly vinaigrette, and cook a few minutes longer. Add salt and pepper, then just before serving toss with basil, chives, and parsley. Serve hot with bread or crostini.

For pasta with clams and mussels, add cooked linguine to the pot the last few minutes and sauté. Serve with a drizzle of olive oil.

patrick's swirly vinaigrette

makes $4^1/2$ cups

1 cup champagne vinegar

$3/4$ cup red wine vinegar

$1/2$ tablespoon saffron, plus a little bit more

2 cups grapeseed oil

$3/4$ cup extra virgin olive oil

salt and pepper to taste

In a saucepan, heat first three ingredients until boiling and vinegars begin to steam. Remove from heat and let cool. Whisk in remaining ingredients.

The vinaigrette is good hot on seafood such as halibut or snapper, or cold on a green salad or tomatoes, with cheese such as feta or aged goat, or with marinated roasted peppers.

le merende
(afternoon snacks)

bread & wine

one portion

2 slices country white bread—
day-old is best

2 tablespoons white sugar

½ cup red table wine

Place the bread on a plate and lightly soak with red wine, so it maintains its shape and is easy to hold. Cover with sugar and ... enjoy!

I remember this afternoon snack with pleasure. I can hear my grandfather telling us kids how healthy that little bit of wine will be for our blood. What a difference in culture!

bread & tomato

one portion

2 slices country white bread

2 very ripe red tomatoes

extra virgin olive oil

salt and pepper to taste

arugula, a little bit, if you have it

red wine vinegar, if you like it

Place the bread on a plate. Cut the tomatoes open and, with your fingers, smash them on the bread, making sure all the juice is absorbed and leaving the chunks of tomato on the bread. Sprinkle with olive oil, salt and pepper, and a few drops of vinegar. Add arugula and sit under your apple tree in good company and enjoy it. One slice will probably not be enough. Healthy, delicate, and ... juicy.

Remember to use your fingers to eat this treat. We were encouraged to use our hands and touch the food, and so we learned to associate the joy of satisfying our appetite with the sense of touch. I remember the food eaten with my hands more, a lot more, than the food eaten in a formal setting!

artichoke dip

serves 6 to 8

2 cups canned artichoke hearts, drained and quartered

2 tablespoons extra virgin olive oil

2 cloves garlic, minced

2 shallots, diced

8 ounces cream cheese, softened

1 cup grated parmigiano

1 cup mayonnaise

1 cup sour cream

dash cayenne

salt and pepper to taste

1 tablespoon chopped italian parsley

2 tablespoons breadcrumbs, for topping

cracker bread, water crackers, or toasted, sliced baguettes

Preheat oven to 375 degrees.

Sauté artichoke hearts, garlic, and shallots in olive oil for a few minutes until artichokes have a little color. Transfer to a mixing bowl and blend with the two cheeses, mayonnaise, sour cream, cayenne, salt and pepper, and parsley. Place in a lightly greased baking dish and sprinkle the top with breadcrumbs. Bake until hot and bubbling—about 25 to 30 minutes. Can be served hot or cold; if cold, omit breadcrumbs. Serve with cracker bread or toasted, sliced baguettes.

As an alternative, slice open a baguette, spoon dip on each side, sprinkle with parmigiano, broil for a few minutes, and serve as a sandwich.

crab & artichoke dip

substitute 1 cup crabmeat for 1 cup artichoke hearts

pinch of old bay spices

pinch each of chopped fresh basil and oregano

Bake and serve as above.

baccelli & pecorino

serves 2

fresh young fava beans in the pod

pecorino toscano

bread

honey

extra virgin olive oil

salt

one bottle red wine

Place fava beans in a beautiful basket. On a cutting board or tray, arrange sliced cheese, sliced bread (or a loaf you can have fun breaking with your hands), honey, olive oil, and salt. Open the fava pods and pick the beans out one at a time, dip them in salt, and eat them with the cheese and bread with a drizzle of honey or olive oil.

Add the company of a man or woman who loves you, a beautiful summer evening, and your favorite wine. Life is made of little things!

fettunta (grilled bread) with cannellini beans & caviar

serves 4

1 14-ounce can cannellini beans
or 2 cups cooked beans
(instructions below)

$1/2$ cup extra virgin olive oil

3 cloves whole garlic

1 roma tomato, halved

a few fresh sage leaves

4 slices day-old country white bread

1 ounce molassol black caviar
(optional)

a few drops fresh lemon juice

salt and pepper to taste

Place drained beans in a soup pot with enough clean water to cover. Add olive oil, 1 clove of garlic, the halved roma tomato, the sage leaves, and salt and pepper. Let simmer 10 to 20 minutes. Drain.

Grill the bread and rub the hot bread with garlic by hand. Spoon hot beans onto the bread. Top with caviar, drizzle with olive oil, a few drops of lemon juice, freshly ground pepper—and oh, this is good!

To cook dried beans, soak 2 cups overnight in 6 cups cold water. The next day, wash and drain the beans, then place them in a soup pot with 6 cups fresh cold water. Add 2 cloves garlic, 4 sage leaves, 1 tablespoon olive oil, and 1 roma tomato. The secret is to cook the beans on a very low flame. My mom says that the beans should not move while simmering! Cover and be patient—bean cooking is not for cooks in a hurry. It takes time (approximately 3 to 4 hours) and love. The best method for judging if they are done is tasting them.

If you go to the trouble of cooking the beans, cook more than you need, and use the remainder tomorrow for soup (see *pasta e fagioli*, p. 75).

The idea of adding caviar to the beans appeared in Florence around the 1800s, and transformed beans from a humble food into something for the illustrious and aristocratic.

high-altitude deviled eggs

makes 24 halves

12 eggs

3 tablespoons mayonnaise

1 tablespoon spicy tarragon mustard

pinch each of salt and white pepper

24 capers

parsley leaves, for garnish

paprika

Place uncooked eggs in enough cold water to cover, then bring to a boil. Turn off heat, cover, and let stand for 13 minutes in the hot water. While still hot, lightly rinse in cold water one at a time. Crack and peel, then cut in half lengthwise. Scoop out the yolks.

Combine the yolks, mayonnaise, mustard, and salt and white pepper. Pipe or scoop the yolk mixture into the white halves. Top with a caper, a parsley leaf, and a dash of paprika.

italian prawns

serves 8

24 to 30 large shrimp, shelled and
   deveined

zest of 1 lemon

pinch of red pepper flakes

$1^1/_2$ tablespoons chopped italian parsley

$^1/_4$ cup extra virgin olive oil, or enough
   to lightly coat the shrimp

$^1/_2$ tablespoon finely chopped garlic

freshly ground black pepper to taste

lemon wedges, for garnish

Cook prawns in boiling salted water until
done—approximately 5 minutes. Drain and
cool.

In a mixing bowl, combine next six ingredients. Toss shrimp in mixture and chill for 30
minutes. Serve cold with fresh lemon wedges
and cocktail sauce. The prawns are also good
hot, tossed with your favorite pasta.

cocktail sauce

1 cup ketchup

$^1/_4$ cup horseradish

juice of 1 lemon

dash of tabasco

$^1/_2$ teaspoon white pepper

1 tablespoon worchestershire sauce

Blend all ingredients together and chill.

artichokes with tomato & shallot topping

artichokes:

for up to 8 artichokes

4 whole cloves garlic

2 whole bay leaves

3 to 6 sprigs fresh thyme

2 lemons, quartered

Trim the stems of the artichokes about 1 inch from the bottom. Place in a large pot with enough water to cover. Add garlic, bay leaves, and thyme. Add lemons after squeezing their juice into the water. Cover, bring to a boil over medium-high heat, and simmer 35 to 45 minutes or until tender. Check by pulling a leaf out of the artichoke and tasting for tenderness. Drain well in colander.

lemon mayonnaise:

makes 1 cup

1 cup homemade or store-bought mayonnaise

zest and juice of one lemon

1/4 cup extra virgin olive oil

1 tablespoon chopped fresh basil

pinch of white pepper

Whisk together and serve.

tomato & shallot topping:

makes 2 cups

1/3 cup extra virgin olive oil

3 cups diced fresh tomatoes

8 shallots, coarsely chopped

1 tablespoon minced garlic

1 tablespoon fresh thyme leaves

salt and pepper to taste

1/2 cup white wine

lemon wedges, for garnish

Heat the olive oil in a sauté pan. Add tomatoes, shallots, and garlic. Cook over medium heat until vegetables are soft. Add thyme and salt and pepper and continue cooking about 5 minutes. Stir in white wine and cook another 2 to 3 minutes.

Spoon 2 tablespoons of the tomato shallot topping over and into the leaves of a cooked artichoke. Garnish with lemon wedges.

Can be served with lemon mayonnaise, if desired.

spicy nuts

makes **2** cups

$^1/_2$ cup sugar

2 tablespoons vegetable oil

2 cups unsalted mixed nuts—pecans, hazelnuts, almonds, cashews, walnuts, brazil nuts

$1^1/_2$ teaspoons cumin

$^1/_2$ teaspoon red pepper flakes

In a sauté pan on low heat, stir sugar and oil with a wooden spoon until sugar is completely dissolved. Add nuts, cumin, and pepper flakes. Toss with the sugar syrup until mixture is golden brown, making sure nuts are completely coated.

With a wooden spoon, transfer the mixture onto a lightly greased cookie sheet. Wearing kitchen gloves (mixture will be very hot), spread and let cool. Store at room temperature.

salads

wild rice & orzo salad

serves 6

1 cup wild rice

$^{1}/_{2}$ pound orzo

4 green onions, sliced in rounds

3 tender stalks celery, diced

1 tablespoon chopped parsley

$^{3}/_{4}$ cup dried cranberries

$^{3}/_{4}$ cup dried apricots, cut in strips

zest and juice of 1 orange

extra virgin olive oil

salt and pepper to taste

Cook the wild rice in boiling, salted water until tender—approximately 45 minutes. Drain and rinse in cold water. Cook the orzo in boiling, salted water until tender—7 to 8 minutes. Drain and rinse in cold water.

In a salad bowl, combine rice and orzo. Add onions, celery, parsley, cranberries, apricots, and orange zest. Mix well. Add orange juice and a few drops of olive oil. Season with salt and pepper.

asparagus & mushroom salad

serves 6

2 bunches asparagus, tough ends removed

2 cups quartered raw button mushrooms (about $1/2$ pound)

Blanch asparagus 1 to 2 minutes in boiling, salted water, then rinse in ice-cold water and drain completely. Slice on the diagonal, then mix with mushrooms.

In a mixing bowl, toss asparagus and mushrooms with enough mustard vinaigrette to coat.

You can add shaved pecorino or parmigiano, red endive for color, or a few leaves of arugula.

mustard vinaigrette

$1/2$ cup vegetable oil

$3/8$ cup rice vinegar

$1/4$ cup dijon mustard

1 tablespoon chopped italian parsley

salt and pepper to taste

Whisk all ingredients together. For tangier flavor, add more mustard. Dressing can be used for green salads, on grilled chicken, or as a dip for crudités.

nunzio's tomato & escarole

serves 4

1 cup escarole

4 vine-ripened or heirloom tomatoes

Wash the escarole and dry in a lettuce spinner or the old-fashioned Italian way—in a towel. Cut tomatoes in wedges and mix with lettuce in a bowl. Add enough dressing to coat, a few leaves of basil, fresh oregano, and freshly cracked black pepper if you like, and it is done.

Tomatoes are best when non-refrigerated. So...always keep your tomatoes at room temperature, cut or whole.

nunzio's dressing

makes 1 cup

$1/2$ cup extra virgin olive oil

2 cloves garlic, minced

2 tablespoons dijon mustard

$1/4$ cup red wine vinegar

salt and pepper to taste

Whisk olive oil and garlic with a fork, smashing garlic on the side of the bowl. Whisk in mustard, vinegar, and salt and pepper.

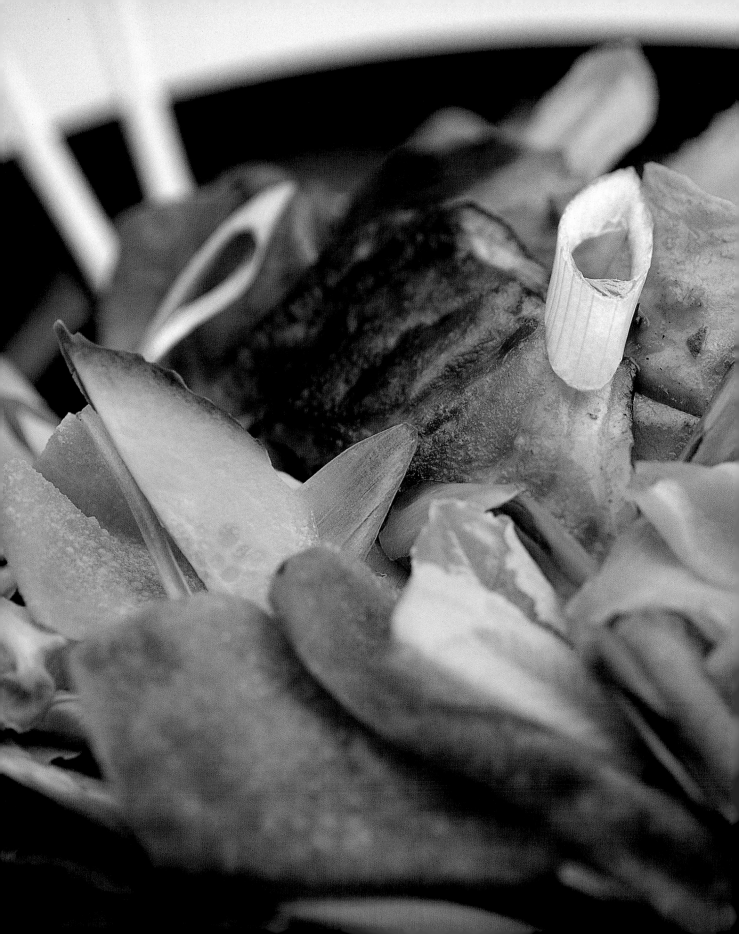

crispy salmon salad

serves 5 to 6

1 fresh salmon fillet, about $2^{1}/_{2}$ pounds

sweet chili sauce

15 wonton wrappers

vegetable oil for frying

1 package radish or clover sprouts

$^{1}/_{2}$ head green cabbage, thinly sliced

a few leaves of basil, sliced

a few leaves of cilantro, sliced

$^{1}/_{2}$ cup green onions, thinly sliced
   on diagonal

1 english cucumber, thinly sliced
   on diagonal

san francisco airport dressing (p. 55)

a few strips of pickled ginger

Slice the salmon in thin strips, coat with the chili sauce, and marinate for at least 30 minutes.

Cut wontons into strips and fry in hot vegetable oil until crisp. Drain on a paper towel.

In a hot, non-stick pan, crisp one batch of the salmon strips, then remove from heat. Repeat until all salmon is cooked.

In a bowl, toss the sprouts, cabbage, basil, cilantro, green onions, and cucumber in the dressing. Plate and top with hot crispy salmon, wonton strips, and a few strips of pickled ginger. Drizzle with more dressing and serve.

celery root salad

serves 2 to 4

2 cups canned celery root, drained
 and shredded, or 6 to 8 fresh
 celery roots

$1/4$ cup black olives, halved

1 tablespoon capers, plus a
 little of their juice

$1/4$ cup tarragon mustard

$1/2$ cup mayonnaise

$1/6$ cup rice vinegar

1 tablespoon chopped italian parsley

black pepper to taste

In a mixing bowl, combine celery root, olives, capers, and juice. Whisk together remaining ingredients and toss with celery mixture to coat.

If you use fresh celery root, peel it first, then shred in a food processor. Drop into a boiling 60/40 solution of water and vinegar, with a pinch each of salt and sugar. Boil 2 to 3 minutes, drain, and dress.

The cooked celery root can be stored in its brine for up to one week.

49

lemon chicken salad

serves 6 to 8

4 cups shredded cooked chicken

zest and juice of one lemon

$^1/_2$ medium red onion, diced

$^3/_4$ cup diced celery

2 tablespoons minced italian parsley

$^1/_3$ cup extra virgin olive oil

1 tablespoon red wine vinegar

$^1/_4$ cup mayonnaise (plain yogurt,
  chicken broth, or more olive
  oil may be substituted)

salt and pepper to taste

Combine all ingredients. For variety, add fresh dill, tarragon, basil, or toasted sliced almonds.

Try this salad on a sandwich with a few leaves of lettuce, on a green salad, as a filling for vine-ripened tomatoes or avocados, or on a piece of toast for breakfast.

michael's tuna sandwich

serves 4 to 6

4 6-ounce cans water-packed
  albacore tuna

1 green onion, chopped

1 teaspoon chopped parsley

1 tender stalk celery, diced

$1/2$ teaspoon dijon mustard

2 teaspoons red vinegar

$1/4$ cup mayonnaise or plain yogurt

1 teaspoon lemon juice (or to taste)

country white bread

Combine all ingredients and mix well. Take two thick slices of Cristina's white bread and…**do not use them**. Instead, scoop tuna mixture onto a bed of greens. Serve immediately and enjoy! Or, if you like, make a sandwich.

san francisco airport salad

serves 8

1 teaspoon tamari or soy sauce

2 eggs

$^3/_4$ cup rice flour

$^1/_2$ cup all-purpose flour

2 pounds uncooked turkey breast,
 cut in thin strips

$^1/_2$ cup sesame seeds, or enough to coat

vegetable oil

2-ounce package saifun or cellophane
 noodles

1 head iceberg lettuce, finely shredded

4 handfuls fresh spinach

$^3/_4$ cup thinly sliced green onions

$^1/_2$ cup cilantro leaves

8 tablespoons chopped peanuts,
 for garnish

san francisco airport dressing

In a bowl, mix tamari and eggs. In a separate bowl, mix the two flours. Dip the turkey strips into the egg mixture, then into sesame seeds, then into the flour mixture. In a large skillet, fry the turkey in hot vegetable oil until crispy and golden. Drain on a paper towel and cool.

In a large skillet, fry saifun noodles in about 2 inches of very hot vegetable oil, a handful at a time. They will puff up immediately. Using a slotted spoon, remove from oil and drain on a paper towel.

In a bowl, gently toss lettuce, spinach, green onions, cilantro, turkey strips, and noodles. Add just enough dressing to coat, garnish with the peanuts, and serve.

san francisco airport dressing

makes 4 cups

1 cup sesame oil

1 cup rice wine vinegar

1 cup soy sauce

$^1/_2$ cup grated ginger

$^1/_2$ cup vegetable oil

$^1/_2$ teaspoon red pepper flakes

$^1/_4$ cup minced garlic

$^1/_4$ cup granulated sugar

Mix all ingredients in a food processor, or whisk together by hand. Let dressing rest overnight—or at least 3 to 4 hours—before serving.

Store any remaining dressing in a covered jar in your refrigerator because it is very good with all salads that come to your mind—hot or cold, vegetarian, meat, or poultry.

italian potato salad

serves 6

18 small red potatoes
$^1/_2$ pound green beans, trimmed
$^1/_2$ small red or white onion, finely diced
extra virgin olive oil
1 tablespoon red vinegar
pinch of chopped fresh basil
2 tablespoons chopped fresh parsley
salt and pepper to taste

Place the potatoes in cold, salted water, and cook until tender. Drain and let cool. Blanch or steam green beans until tender. Drain and cool.

Cut potatoes in wedges. In a large salad bowl, mix the potatoes, green beans, onions, enough olive oil to coat, red vinegar, basil, and parsley. Add salt and pepper to taste. Mix well and serve.

watermelon &
red onion salad

serves **8**

1 medium red watermelon, cut in
  large, irregular chunks

$1^1/_2$ small red onions, cut in
  thin crescents

a few whole leaves fresh mint

1 cup raspberry vinaigrette

feta chunks

Mix all ingredients together in a mixing bowl
and coat with raspberry vinaigrette. Serve
chilled.

raspberry vinaigrette

makes **3** cups

$^1/_3$ white onion, finely diced

1 egg

$2^1/_2$ tablespoons sugar

2 tablespoons dijon mustard

pinch of salt

$^3/_4$ cup champagne vinegar

$^1/_2$ cup fresh raspberries

2 cups vegetable oil

1 tablespoon fresh mint chiffonade

In a food processor, purée onion, egg, sugar,
mustard, salt, and champagne vinegar for one
minute. With the machine running, add raspberries, then the oil in a slow, steady stream
until mixture reaches a creamy consistency.
Add mint chiffonade.

salad niçoise

serves 6

6 handfuls mixed greens (mesclun, bibb, arugula, watercress, or any other green you like)

6 medium vine-ripened tomatoes, quartered

6 small handfuls green beans, steamed or blanched

6 hard-cooked eggs, quartered

6 small red or new white potatoes, boiled and quartered

4 6-ounce cans albacore tuna or 1$^{1}/_{2}$ pounds grilled fresh tuna cut in chunks

$^{3}/_{4}$ cup niçoise olives

18 thinly sliced red onion rings

niçoise dressing

18 anchovy fillets

Toss the greens in a bowl with a splash of dressing. Plate the greens and top with tomatoes, green beans, eggs, potatoes, tuna, olives, and onions. Drizzle with dressing, add anchovies and freshly ground pepper, and serve.

niçoise dressing

makes 1 cup

$^{1}/_{2}$ cup fresh or 2 tablespoons dried oregano

2 cloves garlic, quartered

1 egg or egg substitute

3 tablespoons red wine vinegar

salt and pepper to taste

1 cup extra virgin olive oil

Process all ingredients except olive oil in food processor for one minute. With processor running, add the olive oil in a slow, thin stream to reach a creamy consistency. Adjust seasonings to taste.

shrimp & mango salad

serves 4

4 cups salad greens

12 large prawns, peeled and deveined, grilled or sautéed

3 whole green onions, thinly sliced on diagonal

3/4 cup water chestnuts, drained and sliced

1 ripe mango, peeled and cut in long strips

1 cup citrus-champagne dressing

orange slices, for garnish

Place all ingredients in a mixing bowl and toss with the dressing. Serve on chilled plates garnished with orange slices.

citrus-champagne dressing

makes 2^1/$_2$ cups

1/2 cup champagne vinegar

1 teaspoon orange zest

1/2 cup orange juice

1/2 tablespoon lemon zest

juice of 1/2 lemon

1 tablespoon lime zest

juice of 1 lime

1 cup grapeseed oil

1/4 cup basil oil

1/4 cup grand marnier

Whisk all ingredients together and serve.

soups

tomato bisque

serves 6

3 tablespoons extra virgin olive oil

1 small yellow onion, diced

1 tablespoon finely chopped garlic

2 tablespoons fresh basil chiffonade

$^1/_2$ cup white wine

8 cups fresh, ripe italian tomatoes, diced, with their juice, or 8 cups canned italian tomatoes

$^1/_2$ teaspoon red pepper flakes

salt and pepper to taste

$1^1/_2$ cups cream

fresh basil leaves, for garnish

Sauté onion, garlic, and basil in olive oil until onions are tender and light gold in color. Add wine and let cook a few minutes. Add tomatoes, red pepper flakes, and salt and pepper. Simmer for about 12 minutes, stirring occasionally. Then pulse mixture briefly in a food processor to obtain a creamy consistency.

Return to pot, whisk in cream, and bring to a gentle simmer. Drizzle each bowl of soup with olive oil and garnish with a fresh basil leaf. Serve with crostino of garlic bread.

This soup is very good chilled for a summer evening.

Italians eat a lot of tomatoes. They grow them in their gardens, on their balconies or terraces…everywhere! Inexpensive and multi-purpose, the pomodoro *or "golden apple" is like gold for Italians…precious and indispensable to life.*

hungarian mushroom soup

serves 10 to 12

$1/3$ pound butter ($1^1/4$ sticks)

$2^1/2$ cups onions, cut in crescents

$3/4$ cup flour

$1/3$ cup paprika

$1/3$ cup white wine

16 cups sliced button mushrooms
(about 4 pounds)

$2^2/3$ cups water

$2^2/3$ cups sour cream

$5^1/3$ cups whole milk

$2/3$ cup tamari or soy sauce

$1/3$ cup lemon juice

$1/3$ cup worchestershire sauce

$2/3$ cup chopped italian parsley

$1/3$ cup fresh dill

$1/2$ tablespoon black pepper

3 dashes tabasco

lemon zest, for garnish

Sauté the onions in butter until soft. Add flour and paprika, stirring so the flour does not burn on the bottom of the pan. Cook 5 to 7 minutes—until mixture smells like popcorn.

Add the wine and stir for a few minutes, letting the alcohol evaporate. Add the mushrooms and water. Simmer 10 to 15 minutes or until mushrooms are tender.

Add sour cream, milk, tamari, lemon juice, worchestershire, and parsley. Simmer for about 30 minutes. Stir in dill, black pepper, and tabasco and let sit for a few minutes. Garnish with lemon zest.

Leftover soup makes a great pasta sauce—just mix with pasta and sprinkle with fresh parsley and parmigiano.

Picking wild mushrooms is a ritual in Italy. You have to wear at least one piece of clothing inside out, and carry a basket. Porta fortuna—good luck in finding the mushrooms!

turkey soup with toasted almonds

serves 8 to 10

4 tablespoons butter

1 yellow onion, diced

5 stalks celery, finely diced

2 cloves garlic, chopped

$\frac{1}{2}$ cup flour

12 cups chicken stock

1 quart heavy cream

6 cups shredded cooked turkey

1 cup sliced almonds, toasted

3 bay leaves

2 tablespoons chopped fresh sage

2 tablespoons chopped parsley

salt and pepper to taste

dried cranberries, for garnish

Sauté onion, celery, and garlic in butter until onions are translucent. Add flour and cook on low heat for 8 to 10 minutes, stirring. Gradually whisk in stock and cream. Add turkey, almonds, herbs, and salt and pepper, and simmer slowly for 15 to 20 minutes. Adjust salt and pepper. Garnish with dried cranberries and serve.

Everyone loves this soup! Yes, there is cream…but so what! Don't eat it all!

chicken & barley soup

serves 10

4 tablespoons extra virgin olive oil

1 cup leeks, white part, diced

$1/4$ cup chopped celery

1 cup chopped carrots

1 cup chopped yellow onion

pinch each of fresh thyme and parsley

2 bay leaves

1 teaspoon celery salt

1 teaspoon celery seed

2 zucchini, chopped

2 yellow squash, chopped

1 cup quartered mushrooms (about
  $1/4$ pound)

$2^1/2$ cups shredded cooked chicken

16 cups chicken stock

1 cup barley, washed and drained

salt and pepper to taste

Place olive oil, leeks, celery, carrots, onions, thyme, parsley, bay leaves, celery salt, and celery seed in a large soup pan and cook, covered, for about 10 minutes. Add zucchini, squash, mushrooms, chicken, and chicken stock. Bring to a boil, then add the barley. Cook until barley is tender—about 20 minutes. Adjust salt and pepper and serve.

Should you have soup left over, you may need to add more stock the next day as the barley will absorb liquid.

Beef can be substituted to make beef & barley soup.

pasta e fagioli
(cannellini bean soup)

serves 4 to 6

3 tablespoons extra virgin olive oil

$^1/_2$ cup thinly sliced pancetta (optional)
(about $^1/_4$ pound)

2 cloves garlic, minced

4 cups cooked cannellini beans, with
6 to 8 cups cooking broth (p. 29)

pinch of fresh whole rosemary leaves

3 fresh sage leaves

pinch of red pepper flakes

salt and pepper to taste

$^3/_4$ cup short pasta with holes—
tubetti or maccheroncini

2 ripe tomatoes, quartered

In a soup pan, heat olive oil on low with the pancetta, letting the fat melt into the oil. Add the garlic and sauté for a few minutes, making sure not to burn the garlic. Mash half the beans, leaving the rest whole, and add to the pan. Add rosemary and sage and 6 cups hot cooking broth to start, and simmer for 15 minutes. Add red pepper flakes, salt and pepper, and pasta, stirring so beans do not stick to the bottom of the pan. Add more hot liquid if consistency is too thick. Add the tomatoes. Simmer a few minutes until pasta is done, then serve with a swirl of olive oil and garlic crostini.

Pasta e fagioli *used to be the soup of the peasants and farmers, because it was filling and had protein so they didn't have to buy expensive meat. These days, everyone has discovered the dietary value of beans—not to mention the good taste!*

patrick's
corn chowder

serves 10

$1/4$ pound butter

1 medium red onion, diced

1 tablespoon finely chopped garlic

1 bunch of celery, the white and tender part, diced

3 leeks, the white part, cut in $1/2$ rounds

2 yellow squash, cut in $1/2$ rounds

1 zucchini, cut in $1/2$ rounds

6 small unpeeled red potatoes, each cut in 6 wedges

2 large carrots, peeled and cut in $1/2$ rounds

$2 1/2$ pounds fresh or frozen corn

$1/2$ teaspoon cayenne, or to taste

2 tablespoons chopped italian parsley

$1/2$ teaspoon dried or 1 tablespoon fresh dill

pinch of fresh or dried thyme

pinch of fresh or dried oregano

1 teaspoon celery salt

$1/2$ tablespoon celery seeds

3 bay leaves

salt and pepper to taste

6 cups vegetable stock

2 cups water

1 quart cream

In a soup pot, melt the butter and cook the onions until translucent—about 5 minutes. Add garlic, celery, leeks, squash, zucchini, potatoes, and carrots, and sauté 6 to 8 minutes, stirring a few times. Stir in corn. Add all the remaining herbs and spices and cook 2 to 4 minutes longer. Add the vegetable stock, water, and cream. Cook until vegetables are tender.

Remove from heat and purée half the mixture after removing the bay leaves. Combine the purée with the chunky, stir, and serve.

For a chicken corn chowder, add leftover shredded or grilled chicken. In this case, substitute chicken stock for the vegetable stock.

Italians do not eat many soups made with milk or cream. But this soup is good, and chowders have been a great discovery for me.

lentil vegetable soup

serves 10 to 12

3 tablespoons extra virgin olive oil

2 leeks, white part only, diced

2 shallots, diced

2 medium yellow onions, diced

1 bunch of celery, the white and tender part, diced

2 cups lentils, washed

2 cups stewed, chopped tomatoes, with juice

13 cups vegetable stock or water

4 carrots, peeled and diced

3 parsnips, peeled and diced

6 cloves roasted garlic, minced*

4 bay leaves

1/2 bunch italian parsley, chopped

1 bunch chard, chopped (stems and greens)

Sauté leeks, shallots, onions, and celery in olive oil until golden brown. Add lentils, tomatoes, stock, carrots, parsnips, roasted garlic, and bay leaves. Bring to a boil, then simmer until lentils are tender, approximately 1 hour. Add parsley and chard the last 15 minutes of cooking. Season to taste.

*To roast garlic, cut the top off a whole head, drizzle with olive oil, and season with salt and pepper. Wrap in aluminum foil and bake at 350 degrees for 2 hours. Can be made in advance and refrigerated for up to 6 days.

minestrone

serves 10 to 12

1/2 cup extra virgin olive oil

1 onion, diced

1/2 leek, white part only, cut in 1/2 rounds

2 cloves garlic, minced

1/2 cup diced pancetta (optional) (about 1/4 pound)

3 medium potatoes, cubed

2 zucchini, diced

3 yellow squash, diced

1 large carrot, diced

1 celery stalk with leaves, chopped

1 cup green beans

1 cup peas

handful of chopped kale, stems removed

handful of chopped cabbage

3 cups cooked white beans

1 cup fava beans, if available

pinch each of chopped fresh parsley, thyme, and basil

salt and pepper to taste

6 roma tomatoes, diced

8 cups vegetable stock

2 tablespoons pesto (optional)

grated parmigiano, for garnish

In a soup pot, sauté onion, leek, and garlic in the olive oil for a few minutes. Add diced pancetta, if using. Add the remaining vegetables (except tomatoes), beans, herbs, and salt and pepper. Sauté 10 minutes, stirring with a wooden spoon. Stir in the tomatoes. Add the water or vegetable stock and simmer on low heat for approximately 1 1/2 hours, or until vegetables are tender. Add more hot water if needed.

Serve hot with parmigiano, crostini of bread, or cooked pasta or rice. In Genova they add the pesto just before serving—or you can add it the last 10 minutes of cooking time.

Minestrone is the "sink soup." Use anything you have or like … and have fun with it!

pasta

pomarola
(tomato sauce)

makes 1 quart

1/4 cup extra virgin olive oil

1 small carrot, peeled and coarsely chopped

1/2 onion, red or yellow, coarsely chopped

1 clove garlic, chopped

1/2 stalk celery, coarsely chopped

pinch of fresh parsley

5 basil leaves

salt and pepper to taste

pinch of red pepper flakes

10 very ripe roma tomatoes, chopped

Place all ingredients except the tomatoes in a pot and sauté 6 to 8 minutes. Add the tomatoes with their seeds and juice. Let simmer, covered, until vegetables and tomatoes are soft and juicy. Purée the mixture in a food processor until creamy.

This is the story: There once was a priest who, as we say, had his nose in everything and everywhere. In any affair of the little town where he preached there was il suo zampino—his hands. So, even though he was acting in good faith, the townspeople had a nickname for him—Don Pomodoro. Just like the tomatoes, he was everywhere.

It's the same with this sauce—it is good with everything. On hot bruschetta, fettunta, with pasta (adding a little oil and grated cheese), on meats and fish, on risotto, pizza, on fried eggs in the morning. Or, to make la scarpetta, just heat the sauce and dip your bread in it.

barley risotto

serves 6 to 8

$^1/_2$ cup extra virgin olive oil

4 zucchini, diced

I leek, white part only, cut in $^1/_2$ rounds

2 unpeeled granny smith apples, diced

3 shallots, diced

3 cloves garlic, minced

I$^1/_2$ cups pearl barley

I cup marsala wine

14 cups vegetable stock, heated

I tablespoon chopped fresh sage

I tablespoon fresh thyme leaves

5 fennel seeds

I$^1/_2$ cups arborio rice

salt and pepper to taste

grated parmigiano

In a wide stock pot, sauté zucchini, leek, and apples in $^1/_4$ cup olive oil until gold in color, and set aside.

Sauté the shallots and garlic in $^1/_4$ cup olive oil until the shallots are translucent, taking care not to burn the garlic. Add the barley and stir, cooking until the barley is almost toasted—approximately 5 minutes. Add the marsala wine and $^1/_2$ cup hot vegetable stock. Simmer, stirring, for about 6 minutes or until there is no more liquid in the pan. Stir in the sage, thyme, and fennel.

Add the rice and cook, stirring, for about 2 more minutes. Slowly add the simmering stock, one cup at a time, making sure the liquid is absorbed before adding more. Keep adding liquid until the rice and barley are soft and moist, but not mushy. This should take about 35 minutes. Add the sautéed zucchini, leek, and apples. Serve with freshly grated parmigiano.

bucatini alla carbonara

serves 5 to 6

1 pound bucatini or perciatelli

2 tablespoons butter

1 tablespoon extra virgin olive oil

$^1/_2$ white onion, sliced in thin crescents

$^1/_3$ pound pancetta, thinly sliced and diced

1 teaspoon minced garlic

$^1/_2$ cup white wine

$^1/_2$ cup fresh peas

$^3/_4$ to 1 cup heavy cream

$^1/_2$ cup each grated parmigiano and grated pecorino, mixed together

2 egg yolks (optional)

freshly ground black pepper to taste

Cook bucatini in boiling salted water until al dente—about 10 to 12 minutes.

In the meantime, in a sauté pan over medium heat, sauté onion in butter and olive oil until onion is soft. Add diced pancetta and stir a few times, letting it crisp up—about 7 to 10 minutes. Add garlic, wine, and peas, simmer one more minute, and set aside.

In a serving bowl, combine cream, cheeses, egg yolks (should you decide to use them), and freshly ground black pepper. Mix until creamy.

Drain the bucatini, reserving $^1/_2$ cup cooking water. Add to the cheese mixture and gently combine. Stir in hot pancetta/onion sauce and serve immediately, with more cheese if you like. The pasta should be moist and rich. If not, add a little cooking water or more cream.

There are many variations on this dish. We sometimes add a few sprigs of fresh rosemary or some pepper flakes. Traditionally, there are no peas or wine…but we like them!

pasta & bell peppers

serves 5

8 bell peppers, red, yellow, and orange

2 tablespoons minced garlic

$^1/_2$ cup extra virgin olive oil

$^1/_4$ cup chopped fresh oregano

$^1/_4$ cup chopped fresh italian parsley

$^1/_8$ cup chopped fresh basil leaves

$^1/_2$ cup white wine

1 pound penne

2 cups grated parmigiano or aged pecorino toscano

pinch of red pepper flakes (optional)

salt and pepper to taste

Roast the whole peppers on a cookie sheet in a very hot oven (550 degrees) with a drizzle of olive oil, until soft and the skin is dark and roasted—approximately 20 minutes—turning them a couple of times. Remove from oven and transfer to a mixing bowl. Cover with plastic wrap to steam until cool. When they are cooled, peel, remove the seeds, and save all the juices. Tear the peppers into large chunks and set aside.

In a wide skillet, sauté the garlic in the olive oil. Add the peppers with their juice, the herbs, and the white wine. Simmer for a few minutes.

In the meantime, cook the penne in boiling salted water until al dente. Drain, reserving at least $^1/_2$ cup of the cooking water. Toss the pasta with the pepper sauce in a sauté pan, adding reserved cooking water as needed to moisten. Stir over a high flame for a few minutes. Transfer to a serving bowl, drizzle with olive oil, grated cheese, and freshly cracked pepper.

If you have bread on the table, use it to clean your bowl. It's not good etiquette, but it's good for your soul. Happiness is cleaning your plate and not feeling guilty about it!

tortellini with cream & saffron sauce

serves 4 to 6

3 tablespoons butter

$^1/_2$ cup leeks, white part only, thinly
   sliced in $^1/_2$ rounds

$^3/_4$ cup italian sausage, crumbled

pinch of saffron

pinch of red pepper flakes

I cup heavy cream

I pound tortellini, cheese or spinach

2 egg yolks, lightly beaten

parmigiano

In a saucepan, melt the butter and sauté the leeks until tender and lightly golden. Add crumbled sausage, saffron, and red pepper flakes and let flavor develop on low heat for 8 to 10 minutes. Whisk in the cream and simmer until sauce is creamy and dense, about 5 minutes.

Cook the tortellini in boiling, salted water until al dente. Drain, add to the sauce, and stir together for a few minutes longer. Remove the pan from the heat and gently fold in the egg yolks, mixing well. Add parmigiano and serve immediately.

This sauce is also very good with penne or short fusilli. If you have some left over, place in an oven-proof casserole, add more cheese and a little milk, and gratin at 500 degrees until the top is golden. Serve with a few sautéed or fresh greens.

riccioli with arugula

serves 6

8 large, juicy vine-ripened tomatoes

4 cloves garlic, minced

8 tablespoons extra virgin olive oil

1 cup fresh ricotta or 2 balls fresh
    mozzarella, sliced

3/4 cup chopped basil

2 tablespoons chopped parsley

1/2 red onion, sliced in thin crescents

salt and pepper to taste

1 pound riccioli, or any curly pasta

4 ounces or 4 bunches fresh arugula,
    stems removed

Drop the tomatoes in a pot of boiling water for about 5 seconds. Do not overcook the tomatoes or they will turn to mush. Remove with a slotted spoon and immediately plunge them into a bath of cold water for 5 seconds. Peel off the skin and discard. Dice the tomatoes over the serving bowl so you do not lose any of the juice or seeds.

Gently mix in the garlic, olive oil, ricotta or mozzarella, basil, parsley, onion, and salt and pepper. Marinate for at least 40 minutes.

In the meantime, cook the pasta in boiling, salted water until al dente. Drain and reserve 1/2 cup cooking water. In a large sauté pan, heat 4 tablespoons olive oil, then add the hot pasta and fresh arugula. Mix together for a few minutes on high heat, just until the pasta is very hot and the arugula is wilted. Transfer immediately to the serving bowl with the sauce, and gently mix. Serve, adding a little of the hot cooking water if needed, as the sauce should be loose.

This is what summer is all about! The sauce is called salsa cruda, *meaning "not cooked." You can substitute any herbs you have growing in your garden—tarragon is great, or marjoram, or slivered fresh fennel. Go wild and experiment! As my grandmother said, this sauce is* una benedizione *because it is easy and, most importantly, inexpensive. At least in Greve.*

fettuccine with prawns & chipotle cream sauce

serves 4 to 5

2 tablespoons butter

1 red onion, sliced in thin crescents

6 cloves garlic, slivered

1 yellow bell pepper, diced

16 to 20 large prawns, peeled and deveined

1 handful white sweet corn (about $1/2$ cup)

salt and pepper to taste

6 roma tomatoes, sliced

$1/2$ cup black olives, broken

$1/2$ tablespoon chipotle purée

2 cups cream

1 tablespoon cilantro, whole leaves

2 tablespoons chopped basil

1 pound fettuccine

grated parmigiano

Sauté onion, garlic, and yellow pepper in butter until pepper is soft. Add prawns and sauté for two minutes. Add corn and salt and pepper. Cook for 3 to 5 minutes. Stir in tomatoes, olives, chipotle, cream, cilantro, and basil, then simmer and reduce to blend.

Cook fettuccine in boiling salted water until al dente, and drain. Add sauce, sprinkle with parmigiano, and serve.

spaghetti with artichokes

serves **8**

2 white onions, cut in thin crescents

8 cloves garlic, chopped

5 cups canned artichoke hearts, drained and quartered

$^1/_2$ cup extra virgin olive oil

$^3/_4$ cup white wine

8 cups diced ripe italian tomatoes

$^1/_2$ cup chopped fresh basil

$^1/_4$ cup chopped fresh italian parsley

$^1/_4$ cup chopped fresh oregano

pinch of fresh thyme leaves

1 cup pitted black olives (optional)

2 pounds spaghetti

1 cup grated parmigiano or manchego

In a wide sauté pan on low heat, sauté onions, garlic, and artichoke hearts in the olive oil until tender and gold in color. Add white wine and simmer for a few minutes. Add the tomatoes and simmer slowly, uncovered, for about 1 hour, stirring occasionally. Add herbs and olives, simmer for a few more minutes, and taste for flavor.

Cook pasta in boiling salted water until al dente. Drain, reserving 1 cup of the cooking water.

Add cooked pasta to the sauce and cook on high heat to let flavors come together. Add some cooking water if needed. Sprinkle with cheese and serve with a drizzle of olive oil and fresh basil to garnish.

fish & meat

meat loaf

makes one loaf

2$^1/_2$ pounds ground beef

3 eggs

$^3/_4$ cup breadcrumbs

$^1/_2$ cup grated parmigiano

1$^1/_2$ tablespoons chopped parsley

$^1/_2$ tablespoon minced garlic

1 small yellow onion, finely chopped

pinch of red pepper flakes

salt and pepper to taste

Preheat oven to 375 degrees.

In a mixing bowl, combine all ingredients. Pack firmly into an oiled loaf pan and bake for one hour. To test for doneness, insert a skewer and push, looking for clear liquid.

blackened yellowfin tuna with avocado relish

serves 4

seasoning:

makes about 3 cups

$^1/_2$ cup each chili powder, paprika, onion powder, and garlic powder

4 tablespoons black pepper

$^1/_2$ tablespoon salt

1 tablespoon each cayenne, dried oregano, dried tarragon, white pepper, dried thyme, and dried basil

Mix together all ingredients and store in a jar.

avocado relish:

makes 3 cups

6 vine-ripened or roma tomatoes, diced

$^1/_4$ large white onion, thinly sliced

5 to 8 fresh basil leaves, chopped

1 teaspoon chopped garlic

1 tablespoon extra virgin olive oil

splash red wine vinegar

2 avocados, chopped

salt and pepper to taste

1 ripe mango, cubed (optional)

Gently mix all ingredients together and set aside.

tuna:

4 8-ounce yellowfin tuna steaks

seasoning

2 tablespoons clarified butter per steak

$1^1/_3$ cups avocado relish

Coat the tuna with seasoning, pressing it into the fish, and shake off excess. In a very hot sauté pan oiled with the clarified butter, cook each steak, turning once after one side is crispy—about 2 to 3 minutes per side. Or you can sear the fish in the pan and finish cooking in a 400-degree oven. Serve hot, topped with avocado relish, on a slice of toasted bread or on a bed of greens, with lime wedges to garnish.

swordfish roll-ups

serves **6**

filling:

$^1/_2$ cup currants

$^1/_4$ cup white wine

$^1/_2$ cup extra virgin olive oil

4 large shallots, finely chopped

$^3/_4$ cup fine breadcrumbs

$^3/_4$ cup pine nuts, toasted

pinch of fresh thyme

pinch of chopped parsley

1 teaspoon chopped garlic

$^1/_4$ cup lemon juice

Soak currants in white wine until soft—approximately 15 minutes. Sauté shallots in olive oil until soft and gold in color. Add the remaining ingredients and let cook for 2 minutes, just to mix.

swordfish:

$1^1/_2$ pounds swordfish, cut into 12 slices $^1/_4$-inch thick

$^1/_2$ cup extra virgin olive oil

$^3/_4$ cup white wine

2 tablespoons capers, with juice

2 tablespoons chopped italian parsley

$^3/_4$ to 1 cup vegetable or fish stock

salt and pepper to taste

1 tablespoon lemon zest, for garnish

lemon slices, for garnish

Coat fish lightly with 1 tablespoon olive oil, and place on a cutting board. Spoon 1 tablespoon of filling along the center of each slice and roll up, securing with a toothpick. Reserve small amount of filling for garnish.

In a skillet, sauté the roll-ups in the remaining olive oil on high heat for a few minutes until all sides are golden. Do not overcook. Add the wine, capers and juice, and 1 tablespoon parsley. Simmer 2 minutes. Add enough stock to make sauce for 6 servings. Let cook a few more minutes, taste for salt and pepper. Serve sprinkled with 1 tablespoon parsley, remaining filling, and lemon zest and slices.

chicken enchiladas
with tomatillo sauce

serves 8 to 10

tomatillo sauce:

1 tablespoon extra virgin olive oil

$^1/_2$ tablespoon minced garlic

$^1/_2$ white onion, coarsely chopped

$^1/_2$ green bell pepper, chopped

$^1/_2$ tablespoon cumin powder

$^1/_2$ tablespoon fresh oregano

salt and pepper to taste

2 cups canned diced green chilis,
   with their juice

6$^1/_2$ cups canned diced tomatillos or
   diced green tomatoes

Sauté garlic, onion, bell pepper, cumin, and oregano in the olive oil until soft and golden. Season with salt and pepper. Transfer mixture into a food processor and add chilis and tomatillos. Mix well and set aside.

enchilada filling:

1$^1/_2$ pounds cream cheese, softened

$^1/_4$ cup milk

salt and pepper to taste

4 green onions, sliced in rounds

$^1/_4$ cup fresh cilantro leaves

2 cups shredded cooked chicken

Mix all ingredients together just to blend.

enchiladas:

8 to 10 8-inch flour tortillas, warmed

2 cups grated cheddar cheese

$^3/_4$ cup diced fresh tomatoes, for garnish

fresh cilantro leaves, for garnish

Preheat oven to 375 degrees.

Spoon 2 cups tomatillo sauce into a 13" x 8" oven-proof casserole. Spoon $^1/_2$ cup filling onto each tortilla, along with a little grated cheddar, and roll up. Place enchiladas on top of the sauce. Drizzle extra sauce down the center, sprinkle with cheddar, and bake for about 35 minutes. Serve topped with diced fresh tomatoes and cilantro, and warmed tomatillo sauce.

rack of lamb

serves 6

3 cloves garlic, chopped

4 sprigs rosemary, leaves chopped

4 sprigs sage, leaves chopped

salt and pepper to taste

pinch of mint (optional)

3 racks of lamb, french cut
(approximately 6 to 7 chops per rack)

extra virgin olive oil

$^1/_2$ cup stock or water

Preheat oven to 450 degrees.

Mix rosemary and sage together to make $^1/_2$ cup, and set aside.

Trim very little of the fat from the racks—it is what gives the intense flavor. Rub each rack with olive oil and the herb mixture, front and back, and marinate for a few hours. Heat 1 tablespoon olive oil in an iron skillet large enough to accommodate at least 1 rack. Place the rack in the skillet, fat side down. Sear the meat on both sides until well browned—about 5 minutes. Remove from stove and place on a rimmed, oiled baking sheet. Repeat with the remaining racks.

Add a little stock to the sheet and deglaze with herbs. Place the baking sheet in the pre-heated oven and roast for 4 to 6 minutes longer. Or you can finish on the grill.

Let rest for a few minutes, then cut each chop between the bones and serve. Drizzle with juices. Serve hot from the oven as an entrée or as an appetizer.

chicken pot pie

makes 6

pot pie tops:

sheets of frozen puff pastry

1 egg yolk

3 tablespoons cream or milk

parchment paper

Line a 13" × 18" baking sheet with parchment paper.

Place puff pastry on sheet and thaw. Cut into six equal squares, then brush each square with egg wash (the egg yolk mixed with the cream or milk). Cut a $1/2$-inch-thin strip from each square to use as decoration. Refrigerate flat on baking sheet, wrapped in plastic.

pot pie filling:

$1/2$ pound butter

1 yellow onion, diced

$1/2$ pound button mushrooms, sliced

$1/2$ bunch celery, diced

2 carrots, peeled and diced

$1/2$ cup chopped parsley

1 tablespoon chopped fresh thyme leaves

1 tablespoon flour

$1/2$ cup white wine

3 to $3^{1}/2$ cups milk

6 to 7 small red potatoes, cooked and cubed

cooked meat from two chickens, shredded

1 cup peas

salt and pepper to taste

6 4-inch crocks

Preheat oven to 375 degrees.

In a medium-size pot, melt the butter, then add onion, mushrooms, celery, carrots, parsley, and thyme, and sauté gently until onions are golden. Sprinkle flour over the top and stir, cooking slowly, for about 5 minutes. Gradually stir in wine and milk, and simmer 5 minutes. Add potatoes and chicken, stirring gently, just long enough to let the sauce thicken slightly. Stir in the peas, and adjust thyme and salt and pepper to your taste.

Spoon hot mixture into the crocks, top with chilled pastry, and bake until golden and puffy—20 to 25 minutes.

roasted pork loin with garlic & herbs

serves 6

2$\frac{1}{2}$-pound boneless pork loin, untrimmed

$\frac{1}{4}$ cup dijon mustard

1 teaspoon fennel seeds

6 sprigs fresh rosemary

5 to 6 sprigs fresh sage

6 cloves garlic

10 thin slices pancetta

extra virgin olive oil

salt and pepper to taste

3 apples, cored and cut in chunks

$\frac{1}{2}$ cup apple cider

kitchen string

Preheat oven to 350 degrees.

Butterfly the pork loin: Keeping flat side of knife parallel to cutting board, cut through the loin, unrolling it into a 1-inch-thick rectangular slab. Rub with half the mustard and half the fennel seeds, and horizontally place 3 sprigs of rosemary, 3 sprigs sage, sliced garlic from 3 cloves, and 4 slices pancetta onto the loin. Add salt and pepper and drizzle with olive oil. Roll into a long round and tie with kitchen string. With a sharp knife, make 6 to 7 small incisions in the meat. Into each incision insert a sliver of garlic, a few leaves of rosemary, $\frac{1}{3}$ of a sage leaf, and salt and pepper. Push down with your fingers. Rub with remaining mustard, fennel seeds, olive oil, and salt and pepper.

Heat a few tablespoons of olive oil in a skillet on high heat and sear the loin on all sides, for color and to seal the juices. When golden brown in color—about 10 minutes—remove from the skillet and place in a roasting pan with a few more tablespoons of olive oil, apple chunks, and remaining rosemary, sage, and garlic. Place 4 more slices pancetta on top of the loin, and the rest in the pan around the loin. Roast for about 20 minutes.

Add apple cider to the pan and cook until the inside temperature reaches 135 degrees for rare. Remove the loin from oven and let stand 8 to 10 minutes before slicing, adding more cider if needed. Slice the pork thinly and serve with apple, crispy pancetta, and juices from the pan.

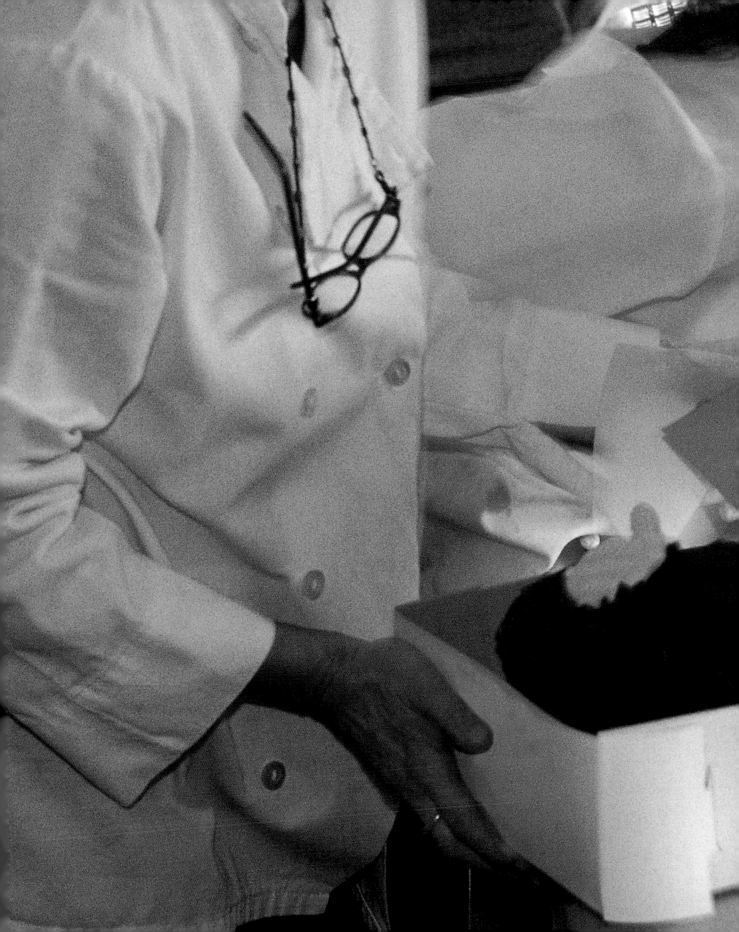

desserts

key lime pie

crust:

3 cups graham cracker crumbs

1 tablespoon vanilla

10 tablespoons melted butter

10-inch springform pan

Preheat oven to 350 degrees.

Combine all ingredients in a bowl. When crumbs are moist, press into the springform pan, pressing up the sides, then the bottom. The sides should be $1^{1}/_{2}$ to 2 inches high.

Bake for 10 minutes or until crust is no longer shiny. Cool completely before filling.

filling:

1 teaspoon gelatin

1 tablespoon water

8 egg yolks

1 cup sugar

$^{2}/_{3}$ cup key lime juice

$2^{1}/_{4}$ cups heavy cream

2 tablespoons key lime zest

Combine water and gelatin in a measuring cup and set aside. Do not stir.

Place yolks, sugar, and key lime juice in a double boiler and whisk gently until thickened. Add the gelatin solution, stir to dissolve, then set aside to cool. Whip the cream to medium peaks and fold into the cooled lime mixture. Add 1 tablespoon zest, then pour into the cooled pie crust. Smooth the top and refrigerate at least 4 hours before serving. Whip additional cream for topping decoration. Garnish with remaining zest.

tiramisu

serves 8 to 10

5 egg yolks

$^3/_4$ cup sugar

2 cups mascarpone

$^1/_4$ cup marsala (a good one, not cooking quality)

$^3/_4$ cup heavy cream

24 ladyfingers

1$^1/_2$ cups hot espresso or strong coffee

$^1/_2$ cup chopped semi-sweet chocolate

Beat yolks and sugar together in a mixer until thick and pale—at least 5 minutes. Add mascarpone and beat until combined. With the mixer still running, add the marsala, then the cream in a slow, steady stream until mixture is creamy and holds peaks.

Spread half the mascarpone cream evenly into a 10-inch glass baking dish. Dip ladyfingers in the espresso, soaking for about 3 seconds on each side, then arrange in a layer on top of the cream. Sprinkle with chocolate chunks, then cover with the remaining cream mixture. Top with remaining soaked ladyfingers in a pattern of your choice, and sprinkle the top with remaining chocolate. Refrigerate at least one hour before serving.

Tiramisu translates as "pick me up"… in the sense of "give me energy"… "make me feel good"… "warm my soul." And so a simple version of this dessert was our breakfast before an important day at school, before a game, or when we were sad. In a coffee cup, whisk 1 egg yolk with 1 tablespoon sugar until pale and creamy, then fill the cup with hot barley coffee, stir, and drink. My grandmother used to say, Bevi che ti fa bene… bevi… bevi.

coconut macaroons

makes 12 to 14

4 packed cups shredded sweet coconut

$^1/_2$ cup sugar

$^1/_2$ cup egg whites

2 tablespoons butter, melted

$^1/_2$ teaspoon almond extract

$^1/_2$ teaspoon vanilla extract

parchment paper

Preheat oven to 350 degrees.

In a mixing bowl, combine all ingredients by hand. Form mixture into pyramid shapes and place on a cookie sheet lined with parchment paper. Bake for approximately 15 minutes or until tops of pyramids are golden. Let cool, then store in an airtight container.

chocolate decadence
(flourless chocolate cake)

makes one 10-inch cake

2 cups chocolate chips

3 tablespoons butter

$^1/_4$ cup espresso

6 eggs

$^3/_4$ cup sugar

1 tablespoon vanilla

10-inch springform pan

parchment paper

Preheat oven to 350 degrees.

Melt chocolate chips, butter, and espresso in a double boiler, then set aside to cool. Separate eggs. Place yolks and sugar in a mixer and whip until pale yellow. Add in the vanilla. By hand, fold the cooled, melted chocolate into the yolks. Whip the whites until stiff, then gently fold into the mixture. Pour into the springform pan lined with parchment paper.

Bake for 30 minutes or until a toothpick inserted in the cake comes out clean. The top will be crusty and may split—don't worry about it! Decorate with chocolate curls or fresh berries.

chocolate curls:

1 cup chocolate chips

2 tablespoons vegetable oil

Combine chocolate and oil together and cook over a double boiler until the chocolate is completely melted. Spread evenly over two cookie sheets, then refrigerate until the chocolate is set.

Remove from refrigerator and warm to room temperature. (If a hand is placed on the sheet, fingerprints should be visible without disturbing the chocolate—they will appear as shiny spots.)

Using the tip of a spatula or putty knife, scrape across the sheet. The chocolate should come up in a strip. Shape into ribbons or curls and use to decorate the top of the cake.

shortbread cookies

makes 12 to 15

$^1/_2$ pound butter, softened

2 cups flour

$^1/_2$ cup powdered sugar

$^1/_4$ teaspoon salt

parchment paper

Preheat oven to 350 degrees.

Combine all ingredients in a mixing bowl and mix until a dough is formed. Roll until $^1/_8$-inch thick and cut into desired shapes. Bake on parchment paper for 8 to 10 minutes or until the shapes are light brown around the edges.

In Italy, the pasticcerie, or pastry shops, which double as cafes, are an important part of our lives. Dolci and dolcezze…fruit tartlets, big-nolini, a frothy cappuccino, winter hot chocolate with cream. Picture marble tabletops and crystal chandeliers…or the more casual ones. Either way they are the center of our social life, political life…and gossip.

In Sun Valley, they could be called body-and-soul warming shops.

colman cookies

makes 16

3 tablespoons butter

1 1/2 cups chocolate chips

1 14-ounce can condensed milk

1 cup flour

1 cup walnuts

parchment paper

Preheat oven to 350 degrees.

Line two 13" x 18" cookie sheets with parchment paper and set aside.

Over a double boiler, melt butter, chocolate chips, and milk, stirring until the chocolate looks shiny and creamy. Do not overheat.

Remove chocolate mixture from stove and quickly fold in flour and walnuts. Scoop the dough onto the prepared cookie sheets, two inches apart, and let rest 15 minutes in a cool place. Bake until tops are cracked—about 9 minutes. Cool before serving.

lemon bars

makes 24

crust:

12 ounces cold butter, cut into
    small pieces

$^3/_4$ cup powdered sugar

3 cups flour

Preheat oven to 350 degrees.

Mix crust ingredients in a food processor just
enough to blend. Pat and spread dough
about $^1/_8$-inch thick onto the bottom and up
the sides of a 13" x 18" cookie sheet. Be
careful not to overwork the dough—you
want it to stay cool. Bake until light golden—
approximately 10 to 15 minutes. In the
meantime, prepare filling.

filling:

1 teaspoon baking powder

4 cups granulated sugar

8 eggs

$^1/_2$ cup plus 2 tablespoons lemon juice

zest of 3 lemons

In a mixing bowl, combine baking powder
and sugar. Stir in eggs with a wooden spoon
and set aside.

When crust is done, remove it from oven.
Add lemon juice and zest to filling mixture
and immediately pour into the baked crust.
Bake about 25 minutes or until firm to the
touch. Cool, then cut into squares and dust
with powdered sugar.

For lime bars, substitute lime or key lime
juice for the lemon juice.

Serve the bars with strawberries macerated
in lemon juice and sugar, and a dollop of
whipped cream.

limoncello

8 lemons from your garden lemon tree

4 cups or 1 liter 95-proof ever clear alcohol, or 100-proof vodka

2 pounds plus $^1/_4$ cup sugar

4 cups water

$2^1/_2$-quart lidded glass jar

cheesecloth

Zest the lemons in long strips, without the white part. Infuse the zests in the alcohol for four days in the glass jar, stirring once in a while.

When ready, heat the 4 cups of water in a saucepan. Add sugar and stir until it dissolves and reaches the consistency of thin syrup (190 to 200 degrees on a candy thermometer). Cool completely. Add the syrup to the lemon-and-alcohol infusion and let rest again for eight days. Filter through cheesecloth and pour back into the jar. Refrigerate.

Serve cold with a twist of lemon.

My father loves his lemon trees. They are always lined up outside in terra cotta pots in the summer, and protected inside in the winter. I have seen the making of this rosolio al limone *many times. We all love it and our excuse for drinking it is that it helps the digestion!*

mixed fruit tart

crust:

2$\frac{1}{2}$ cups flour

$\frac{1}{4}$ teaspoon salt

1 teaspoon sugar

$\frac{1}{2}$ pound unsalted butter, chilled
   and cut into small pieces

$\frac{1}{4}$ to $\frac{1}{2}$ cup ice water

10-inch tart pan with a removable
   bottom

In the bowl of a food processor, combine flour, salt, and sugar. With the motor running, blend in pieces of butter until the mixture resembles coarse meal. Slowly add the ice water until the dough holds together. If the dough is too crumbly, add a little more ice water. Form into a ball, wrap in plastic, and refrigerate for 30 minutes.

Roll the chilled dough on a lightly floured board to form an 11-inch circle. Place into the tart pan, which has been lightly buttered and dusted with flour. Set the pan on a baking sheet, then press the dough into the bottom edges and along the sides. Trim the dough $\frac{1}{2}$ inch higher than the edge of the tart pan and fold the excess to the inside of the pan. Chill 15 to 20 minutes.

Preheat oven to 375 degrees.

Line the crust with aluminum foil, pressing it gently into the corners and edges, and cover it with dried beans for weight. Bake until edges begin to color—18 to 20 minutes. Remove the beans and foil and continue to bake until the pastry turns a rich, golden color. Cool completely on a rack before filling.

fruit filling:

2 tablespoons raspberry jam or
   orange marmalade to glaze

1 tablespoon water

cointreau or brandy (optional)

1 pint raspberries

2 peaches, sliced

1 pint strawberries

1 pint blueberries

Heat the jam, water, and cointreau in a saucepan until warm and liquid. Combine all the fruit in a mixing bowl, and gently toss with the jam mixture. Mound loosely into the baked tart shell, remove rim of tart pan, and serve.

The most charming way to end a summer meal is with frutti di bosco—*fruits from the woods. Arrange them in a beautiful cup and splash them with spumante or a drop of balsamic vinegar. Freeze them for a few minutes and serve as a* semifreddo—*semifrozen* delizioso! *What about ripe peaches? Slice them and drown them in good red wine. Let them rest for a second and then…we talk! What a dessert!*

panna cotta

serves 8 to 10

2¹/₂ teaspoons gelatin

¹/₄ cup milk

2 vanilla beans

3 cups heavy cream, 1 cup set aside

2 cups powdered sugar

¹/₂ teaspoon salt

1¹/₂ cups sour cream

Whisk together gelatin and milk and set aside. Slit open vanilla beans and scrape vanilla into 2 cups heavy cream, then drop in the bean shells. Heat cream, add powdered sugar and salt, and stir until powdered sugar dissolves. Whisk in gelatin mixture and heat until gelatin dissolves. Remove bean shells and place the mixture in an ice bath.

Whip remaining cup heavy cream until stiff peaks are formed.

Whisk sour cream into the vanilla mixture until no lumps are visible. Fold in whipped cream. Pour into a 9" x 9" glass serving dish and refrigerate for at least 4 hours.

Serve with fresh berries, puréed fresh fruit, or caramel or chocolate sauce.

ricotta & cioccolato

serves **4**

1^1/$_2$ cups fresh ricotta

3 tablespoons sugar

^{1}/$_2$ tablespoon cocoa powder

wafer cookies

splash of sambuca

In a mixing bowl, blend together ricotta, sugar, and cocoa powder with a fork. Spoon mixture onto each plate and garnish with wafer cookies and a drop of sambuca.

You can substitute espresso powder for the cocoa, and garnish with chocolate-covered coffee beans and sambuca.

CRISTINA'S

Marmellata Di Pr...

KETCHUM IDAHO

green tomato jam

makes three 9-ounce jars

2½ pounds green tomatoes
1 pound sugar
zest and juice of one lemon
pinch of white pepper

Cut the tomatoes in chunks and place them with their juice and seeds in a stockpot with a splash of lemon juice. Cook on low heat, stirring frequently, until tomatoes are very soft—about 30 minutes. Remove from heat and purée in a food processor. Transfer the purée back to the pot and add sugar, lemon juice, and lemon zest. Simmer gently, stirring, until jam consistency is reached—about 1 hour. Add white pepper and cook, stirring, 8 to 10 minutes.

Transfer to clean jars, and seal and sterilize according to manufacturer's instructions.

This is my Aunt Nella's recipe. She never, never threw anything away and so...this was her way to use the end-of-summer, never-ripened tomatoes. It will bring a few summer memories back during those cold winter days....

breakfast

scones

makes 6

2$\frac{1}{2}$ cups flour

1 tablespoon baking powder

$\frac{1}{2}$ cup sugar

lemon or orange zest

10 tablespoons butter, chilled

1 cup heavy cream

$\frac{3}{4}$ cup fresh, dried, or candied fruit
   (cranberries, currants, or cherries)

parchment paper

Preheat oven to 375 degrees. Line a cookie sheet with parchment paper and set aside.

Mix together flour, baking powder, sugar, and zest. Cut in the chilled butter until mixture resembles coarse meal.

Stir in cream and fruit, mixing just until the dough holds together. If using fresh fruit, fold in by hand.

Turn the dough onto a lightly floured board and shape into a slightly domed shape. Cut into 6 wedges, sprinkle with sugar, and bake for 15 to 20 minutes.

bran muffins

makes 12

1 cup hot water

$3^{1}/_{2}$ teaspoons baking soda

$^{1}/_{2}$ cup solid vegetable shortening

1 cup sugar

2 eggs

2 cups buttermilk

$2^{1}/_{2}$ cups flour

2 cups all bran cereal

2 cups whole wheat unprocessed
    bran flakes

1 cup golden raisins

$1^{1}/_{4}$ cups chopped walnuts (optional)

$1^{1}/_{2}$ cups pitted prunes, halved

pinch of salt

Add baking soda to hot water and set aside. In a mixing bowl, cream shortening and sugar until smooth. Add eggs one at a time, lightly mixing after each addition. Without stirring, add all remaining ingredients, including water/baking soda mixture. When all ingredients are in the bowl, mix by hand just to combine—do not over-mix.

Let rest 4 hours or overnight in refrigerator.

Preheat oven to 350 degrees.

When ready to scoop, do not stir muffin mix. Scoop from top, placing $^{3}/_{4}$ cup of muffin mix into a lightly oiled standard muffin pan. Bake approximately 45 minutes. The mix stores for at least five days—make a batch and use when needed.

orange cranberry muffins

makes 8 to 10

2 cups flour

$^{1}/_{2}$ teaspoon salt

1 cup sugar

$^{1}/_{4}$ cup butter

zest of one orange

2 eggs

1 cup buttermilk

1 teaspoon baking soda

1 12-ounce bag fresh cranberries

juice of one orange

Preheat oven to 350 degrees.

Mix together flour and salt and set aside. In the large bowl of a mixer, cream sugar, butter, and orange zest, then add the eggs one at a time. In a separate bowl, combine the buttermilk and baking soda. With the mixer running, alternately add half the buttermilk solution and half the dry ingredients to egg mixture. Repeat, then fold in the cranberries by hand. Fill lightly oiled muffin tins half full and bake for 15 to 20 minutes. Remove from oven and brush the tops with orange juice while they are still hot.

turkey hash

serves 6 to 8

3 pounds medium red potatoes

1 teaspoon paprika

salt and pepper to taste

extra virgin olive oil

2 medium yellow onions, cut in thin crescents and caramelized*

2 pounds oven-roasted turkey breast, shredded

4 tablespoons whole grain mustard

3 cups fresh spinach

1 or 2 poached eggs per serving (optional)

Preheat oven to 375 degrees.

Place whole potatoes in plenty of cold, salted water, bring to a boil and cook until firm. Drain, and cool. Cut each potato into 4 wedges and place on a lightly oiled cookie sheet. Season with paprika, black pepper, and a pinch of salt. Drizzle with olive oil to coat, then crisp them in the oven for 30 to 45 minutes until golden, but not dry.

In a large sauté pan on medium heat, add the potatoes, caramelized onions, turkey, and mustard. Stir in spinach, then turn up the heat and let spinach wilt. When the mixture is hot, serve topped with poached eggs, or just the way it is. The hash should be moist; if not, stir in a little hot water or stock.

*To caramelize the onions: In 2 tablespoons olive oil with a pinch of pepper, sauté onions, covered, over high heat until juices start to release. Then on low heat, uncovered, stir every so often until gold in color—30 to 45 minutes or longer.

breakfast gnocchi

serves 4

1 pound potato gnocchi, fresh
  or frozen

5 tablespoons butter

8 to 10 eggs

salt and pepper to taste

2 tablespoons water

1 cup crispy bacon bits

3 tablespoons sliced green onion

grated parmigiano

Have two sauté pans ready on the stove—one for the gnocchi, one for the eggs.

Sauté gnocchi in 4 tablespoons butter until golden brown. Mix the eggs in a bowl with salt and pepper and water. Add the remaining tablespoon of butter to the egg pan and heat, then add the egg mixture and start to scramble. While the eggs are still soft, add the bacon bits and onions.

Before the eggs are completely done, fold in the golden hot gnocchi. Stir, adjust seasoning, and serve sprinkled with parmigiano. Do not overcook the eggs—they should be soft and fluffy.

savory brown-butter crepes

makes 16 to 18

2 tablespoons butter, browned

2 eggs

1 1/2 cups flour

1 3/4 cups milk

1/2 cup water

pinch of salt

pinch of any herbs you like (optional)

sweet brown-butter crepes

same as brown-butter crepes but omit salt and herbs, and add:

1 tablespoon sugar, brown or granulated

1/2 teaspoon vanilla

1 tablespoon flavored liqueur such as orange, lemon, or brandy

To brown butter, melt in a skillet until it smells like popcorn and is gold in color but not burned.

In a mixing bowl, whisk together browned butter, eggs, flour, milk, water, and salt and herbs (or sweet ingredients) for 30 seconds.

Brush a 6- to 7-inch non-stick skillet with oil or melted butter and heat on medium until hot. Remove from heat and, holding the skillet, pour 1/8 cup of the crepe mixture in the middle. Tilt the skillet in all directions so the batter covers the bottom in a thin layer. Return skillet to heat for about 1 minute. Lift edges with spatula; if the underside has gold speckles, turn the crepe over. Let cook until gold speckles appear, then slide crepe onto a plate and repeat the process with the remaining batter. Keep warm if to be used immediately, or store for later. Reheat stored crepes in foil in the oven for soft crepes, or on a baking sheet for lightly crispy.

mascarpone & nutella filling for crepes

makes enough for 6 crepes

3/4 cup mascarpone

3/4 cup nutella (italian chocolate spread available in stores)

powdered sugar to sprinkle, or hot chocolate sauce

Loosely spread 2 tablespoons each of mascarpone and nutella into a warm, sweet brown-butter crepe. Fold or roll the crepe, sprinkle with powdered sugar or hot chocolate sauce, and eat it slooooooooowly…savoring every single bite!

You have lots of options for fillings: good jam with fresh fruit, cooked apples and cream, raisins and nuts, figs with a drizzle of port, sambuca, or vino santo.

spinach gruyère filling for crepes

serves 6

12 savory brown-butter crepes (p. 153)

2 pounds fresh spinach

4 tablespoons extra virgin olive oil

1 large white onion, diced

1 tablespoon diced garlic

2 tablespoons fresh thyme leaves

pinch of red pepper flakes

pinch of grated nutmeg

2 cups grated gruyère (about $^{1}/_{2}$ pound)

1 cup grated parmigiano

1 tablespoon chopped parsley

2 cups white sauce

salt and pepper to taste

6 roma tomatoes, for garnish

Preheat oven to 375 degrees.

Blanch the spinach in hot, salted water for 2 minutes. Wring out the water, chop, and set aside.

Sauté the diced onion in the olive oil until translucent, then add garlic, thyme, red pepper flakes, and nutmeg. Cook until onions are soft. Add the chopped spinach, sauté for a few more minutes, then remove from heat and set aside.

In a bowl, mix cheeses, parsley, white sauce, and salt and pepper. Fold in spinach mixture.

Cut the tomatoes in half lengthwise. Sprinkle with salt and pepper. In a non-stick sauté pan, heat a few drops of olive oil and, on high heat, quickly sauté the tomatoes, skin up, until gold in color. Turn tomatoes skin down and heat for one minute. Set aside.

Place crepes on a cutting board or table. Spoon the filling into the center of each crepe, then loosely fold crepe edges to the center, like a flower. Place the crepes in a buttered baking dish and bake until edges are crispy—about 10 to 15 minutes. Transfer to a serving plate and drizzle with white sauce and cheese. Garnish with 2 charred tomato halves per plate.

white sauce for crepes

makes 2 cups

$^{1}/_{4}$ pound butter

$3^{1}/_{2}$ to 4 tablespoons flour

2 cups milk

$^{1}/_{2}$ white onion, uncut, for flavor

1 clove

1 bay leaf

pinch of nutmeg

pinch of white pepper

1 fennel seed

Melt the butter on low heat. Whisk in the flour and blend until mixture smells like popcorn—2 to 3 minutes. Slowly whisk in milk. Add the onion, clove, bay leaf, nutmeg, white pepper, and fennel seed and stir over low heat until thick and smooth. Discard the onion and clove. Strain the mixture through a fine strainer. Add a little more milk if you like a looser consistency.

frittata with swiss chard & onions

serves 4 to 6

1 tablespoon butter

2 tablespoons extra virgin olive oil

2 cups white onions, cut in
 thin crescents

1½ cups coarsely chopped swiss chard

½ teaspoon minced garlic

pinch of chopped parsley

pinch of chopped thyme

pinch of salt and pepper

6 eggs

1 tablespoon water

1 cup fresh baby spinach

½ cup grated pecorino or parmigiano

In an 8-inch non-stick skillet on low heat, sauté onions in butter and 1 tablespoon olive oil until translucent and light gold in color—about 10 minutes. Add swiss chard, garlic, parsley, thyme, and salt and pepper. Cook 5 to 6 minutes, stirring occasionally, until the chard is wilted.

In a bowl, lightly beat eggs and water. Add the onion/chard mixture. In the skillet, heat remaining tablespoon olive oil over medium heat. When the oil is hot, pour in egg and vegetable mixture. Lower the heat and, lifting up the sides with a spatula, let uncooked egg mixture slide under to firm up. Cover and continue to cook until just a little loose egg mixture is visible on top—about 5 to 6 minutes.

Carefully invert frittata onto a large plate and return to skillet, browned side up. Cook second side until golden—about 1 minute. Transfer frittata to a plate, cut into wedges, and serve topped with fresh spinach tossed in vinaigrette and grated cheese.

Frittatas are a great way to use leftovers—from pasta to sausages, green tomatoes, and meats. Excellent for a light Sunday supper with salad and bread. As with many Italian dishes, the frittata comes from very humble traditions. It is basically an egg pie, and you cannot go wrong!

index